How to Help Your Friends

by
Joe E. Richardson, Jr.

CONVENTION PRESS
Nashville, Tennessee

This book is the text for course number CG-0134
in the subject area "Ministry"
in the Christian Growth category of the Christian Growth Study Plan.

Dewey Decimal Classification Number: 248.83
Subject Heading: YOUTH–RELIGIOUS LIFE/DISCIPLESHIP
/FRIENDSHIP

Unless indicated otherwise, all Scripture quotations are from the *New American Standard Bible.* © The Lockman Foundation, 1960, 1962, 1963, 1968, 1971, 1972, 1973, 1975, 1977. Used by permission.

See *DiscipleYouth Bible,* Holman Bible Publishers, 1985.

Verses marked NIV are from the Holy Bible *New International Version,* copyright © 1973, 1978, 1984 by International Bible Society. Used by permission.

Verses marked KJV are from the King James Version.

Printed in the United States of America
Available from Customer Service Center, 1-800-458-BSSB
and Baptist Book Stores.

Youth Section
Discipleship and Family Development Division
The Sunday School Board of the Southern Baptist Convention
127 Ninth Avenue, North
Nashville, TN 37234-0152

CONTENTS

THE WRITERS

Joe Richardson, writer of the Content is a certified counselor and a psychologist. He has served on the faculties of Texas A & M University, College Station, Texas, and Midwestern State University, Wichita Falls, Texas. He received counselor certification from Sam Houston State University, Huntsville, Texas. He currently serves as a Christian psychologist in private practice in Nacogdoches, Texas.

Karen Dockrey, writer of the Group Learning Activities has served as youth minister in paid and volunteer positions. She currently spends her professional time writing for youth and their leaders. She leads conferences across the nation. She volunteers with youth at Bluegrass Baptist Church in Hendersonville, Tennessee. She is a graduate of Southern Baptist Theological Seminary. Her books include the *Holman Student Bible Dictionary.*

INTRODUCTION

Perhaps the most important characteristic of any friendship is the willingness to help one another. A friend is a person willing to help when help is needed, but sometimes the problem comes in knowing just how to help. This book is designed to help you know how to help your friends.

Each session in this book covers a different aspect of the process of helping. The first session, "How to Sense Problems," is designed to help you improve your skills for sensing when your friends are hurting. If you are the kind of person who often has friends to call and confide their troubles, you are probably already a good listener. But we can all improve as a listener. We will look at several signs of distress. And you will gain insight into how to control your emotions.

The second session, **"How to Confront Problems,"** will help you learn how to confront the problem without unnecessarily hurting your friend.

The third session, **"How to Help Friends Work Through Their Problems,"** is the heart of what this book is about. In it you will learn some skills for using your life to help someone else. This is what the Christian life is. Christ spent His earthly ministry giving us a model for effectively helping others.

The fourth session, **"How to Follow God as a Guide,"** will help you connect your developing discipleship as a Christian to your daily life in the real world.

The final session, **"How to Use the Bible to Address Today's Problems,"** strives to show you how to find help in the Bible for the problems your friends face.

Something for Later

At the end of each session is "Something for Later." Use these devotional thoughts and brief Bible studies in your quiet time during the following week. If you have *DiscipleHelps: A Daily Quiet Time Guide and Journal,* use the section beginning on page 7 to record additional thoughts.

A final word. This is not a book for you to just read. Instead, it is written in a way to encourage you to share and participate. With a little effort on your part, God will honor your desire to help your friends.

Extra

Recent Suicide Leaves Confusion

ANYTOWN, USA — Last month's sudden and tragic death of Chad Smith left his parents, Mr. and Mrs. John Smith, distraught and confused. Neither seemed to have had any warning of their son's plan.

According to his father, Chad was a quiet, reflective boy. "He spent most of his time in his room with the door closed. Playing with his computer, I think," said Smith. "Chad was always quiet, much more than his friends. He seldom laughed or seemed to be having fun."

"I guess Chad always appeared a little sad. No, maybe serious is the best word. He always took life so seriously. But we had no idea that he would consider taking his life," added Mrs. Smith.

Chad's parents were not alone in their surprise and confusion. Warren Adams, probably Chad's closest friend since the third grade, expressed the same thoughts. "Chad had recently been having some trouble in algebra and chemistry; but, gee, we all were. I guess that was a new experience for him because he usually did so well in school. He had his heart set on getting into a good college. He was afraid his grades might keep him out."

Warren went on to say that Chad's recent problem with his grades seemed to be causing some trouble with Chad's girlfriend, Sue Adams.

"We were always arguing over little, picky things that really didn't matter. He was so concerned with his college choice, like the whole world hinged on where he went to school. But I never once thought he was serious enough to. . . ."

Her voice trailed off as she fought back tears. Then she continued, "None of us thought he was that worried. We should have known."

How to Sense Problems

But Jesus knew what they were thinking (Luke 6:8a, NIV).

Unscramble the following phrase to learn the most important characteristic of any friendship.

insignswell ot phel

Supply the correct vowels to learn the first step in the process of being able to help others. Individual words are separated.

s ns ng/th t/th r / s/ /pr bl m

Chad never talked about his thoughts of suicide with Sue or Warren.

What Did You Say?

Listening is necessary for sensing when a friend has problems. But seldom are we taught how to listen. Think about it. Your mom and dad spent hours teaching you to talk. Your school teachers worked hard to teach you to read and write. But, everyone just expected you to know how to listen.

1. A good listener is p _____ .

Avoid trying to rush the story (even if you're bored or have something else to do).

Read *Exodus 18:13*. One of Moses' duties was to listen to the problems of the Israelites and give them instructions about what they should do. Can you imagine about a million people whining and fussing, and having to listen all day long? That took patience.

2. A good listener tries to u_____ .

3. A good listener applies w_____ .

Wise Young Man

Read *1 Kings 3:7-12,16-28*. King Solomon was known for his wisdom. He often had to make difficult decisions for the Israelite people.

1. According to this passage Solomon was (check one)

❑ an old man.

❑ a young guy.

2. Where did he get his wisdom?

3. Name a difficult decision he had to make.

What is the toughest decision you have helped a friend make? Did you offer good advice? What was your advice?

4. A good listener risks being s_____.

An idea well-expressed is like a design of gold, set in silver. A warning given by an experienced person to someone willing to listen is more valuable than gold rings or jewelry made of the finest gold (Prov. 25:11-12, GNB).[1]

We earn the right to advise our friends by listening to them first.

Dodging Roadblocks

Roadblock behavior by a listener can stop someone from trying to talk about painful experiences.

When was the last time you overreacted to a situation? How did you feel at the time?

Why do you
think you overreacted?

Breaking Barriers

What is one way you have been a barrier to communication?

Riding the Roller Coaster:
Five Signs Of Distress

Your emotions are like a roller coaster. Some emotional behaviors may become more frequent. When they do, they serve as warning flags that trouble could be just around the bend.

Acting out.

Acting out is a term that describes what kind of behavior?

Withdrawal

Withdrawing is the same thing as being shy.
True/False

Sudden, unexplained mood swings.

Yes, some mood changes are normal during the teen years. But other mood swings seem big, even for teenagers.

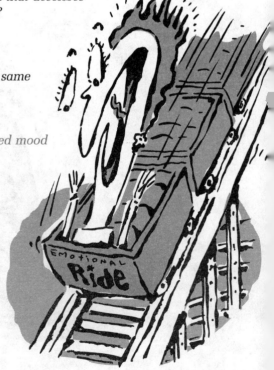

When could there be a problem?

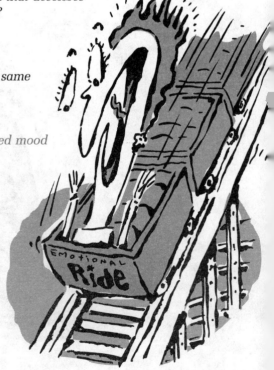EMOTIONAL Ride

Major life problems.

Rank the following events in "stressed order" (1 being the most stressful and 10 being the least stressful).

❑ NOT MAKING A TRYOUT OR AUDITION

❑ DIVORCE OF YOUR PARENTS

❑ MAKING A LOW GRADE ON A REPORT CARD

❑ MOVING

❑ HEALTH PROBLEMS

❑ BAD HAIR DAY

❑ FAMILY FINANCIAL PROBLEMS

❑ TAKING EXAMS

❑ BREAKING UP WITH A BOYFRIEND/GIRLFRIEND

❑ DEATH OF A PARENT

Depression.

Depression is not the same as occasionally being "down."

When could depression be a warning sign?

You Are Not Alone

Write a prayer to God. Thank Him for loving you and giving you guidance when you have needed it. Ask Him to help you develop the patience, understanding, and wisdom to become a Christian helper for your friends.

Something for Later

CONSIDER USING THE FOLLOWING DEVOTIONAL THOUGHT
THIS WEEK IN YOUR QUIET TIME.

Jesus had begun traveling through the area we now call the Middle East. On His travels, He gained followers and enemies. For all those who wanted their families and friends to hear Him, there were others who wanted to trick Him into breaking the law.

One of those trap situations is recorded in the Book of Matthew *(Matt. 22:33-40)*. Jesus had been teaching a large group of people. They were impressed with His teaching. However, there were some members of the Pharisees present who weren't. They feared His message and resented His popularity.

To get Jesus to say something they might use against Him, one of the Pharisees, a lawyer, asked him, *"Which is the great commandment in the Law?"*

Jesus answered with two commandments around which the whole Bible revolves. First, He quoted *Deuteronomy 6:5* saying, *" 'You shall love the Lord your God with all your heart, and with all your soul, and with all your mind.' "This is the great and foremost commandment."*

Then, He continued by quoting part of *Leviticus 19:18,* *"The second is like it, 'You shall love your neighbor as yourself.' "*

In the process of helping your "neighbor," be sure to keep these commandments in mind.

How can you show your love for God this week?

Who do you know that needs to experience God's love in a special way?

ERICA BROWN IS IN TROUBLE

Suppose one of your best friends, Erica Brown, comes to school on Friday with a splitting headache. The night before, after the school play in which Erica had a staring role, she and two other cast members decided to celebrate their performance. They found some vodka in the Brown's liquor cabinet and mixed themselves a drink to relax. Several "relaxations" later, they were smashed. The three fell asleep in the den. Erica's parents were away on business and would not be home until the next day.

Erica shows up at school at noon. She tells you the whole story. Because of last night's events, she hasn't done her math homework; therefore, she wants to borrow yours. She also has not studied for her American History exam. Her math and history classes are sixth and seventh periods. She asks you to tell your fifth period English teacher that she is sick so that she can have time to study for the exam and to copy your math homework.

How do you handle her requests? What do you say and do? This is not the first time Erica has come to school with headaches or that she has asked you to cover for her. She seems to be having more and more trouble on Monday mornings.

What would you do?

How to Confront Problems

"If your brother sins, go and reprove him in private" (Matt. 18:15a).

Help!

Are you involved in a program that helps others? Does your school or church youth group do anything to help solve the problems that students face? Place a check in the box beside those issues that are being addressed.

School		Youth Group
☐	Substance abuse	☐
☐	Designated driver program	☐
☐	Domestic abuse	☐
☐	Loss of family income	☐
☐	New to community	☐
☐	Suicide prevention	☐
☐	Learning problems	☐
☐	Divorce of parents	☐

FIVE THINGS YOU MAY CONFRONT
WHEN YOU TRY TO HELP YOUR FRIENDS

Confrontation 1 – FACING THE FACTS
What do you do when a friend tries to get you to do something you know to be wrong or dangerous, or maybe something that you just do not wish to do?

Confrontation 2 – DEALING WITH DEALERS
What do you do when you suspect that your friend is involved in substance abuse?

Confrontation 3 – FACING UP TO UNFAIRNESS
What do you do when you are faced with the unfair beliefs of your friends?

Jesus Spoke Up

Jesus, our model for all relationships, confronted problems. Read each of the following Scripture passages and record the name(s) of the person(s) confronted and the problem.

SCRIPTURE	PERSON(S) CONFRONTED	PROBLEM
Matthew 9:1-8		
Matthew 14:25-33		
Mark 2:15-17		
Mark 10:35-45		
Luke 10:38-42		
John 20:24-31		

Based on what you have read in these passages, Jesus confronted:

a. enemies
b. strangers
c. friends
d. all of the above

Confrontation 4 – DEALING WITH DENIAL
What do you do when you confront a friend and he denies that he has a problem?

A Very Ugly Story

The Bible reveals the ugly side of human beings and the beauty and goodness of God. One of the uglier stories involves David.

According to *2 Samuel 12:1-11* how did Nathan confront David's problem?

Confrontation 5 –
HELPING UNDER FIRE
What do you do when a
friend verbally attacks you?

Most of the time when someone angrily "chews me out" I:

❑ lash back.   ❑ quickly withdraw.

"If your brother sins, go and reprove him in private" (Matt. 18:15a).

The Christian thing to do is accept the friend and work to help remove the problem behavior.

Three-Part No

Another way to stay out of a bad situation is to respond the **Three-Part No.** To try it, follow these three steps:

1. Say "NO!" rather than any other phrase that could be taken the wrong way.

2. Tell your friend why.

3. Finally, if there is something you can do to help your friend, be sure to say what that is.

The **Three-Part No** can be thought of in these words: No, because . . ., but if . . . .

Write a response to each of the following requests:

A friend wants to borrow your car (actually your dad's) to run an errand; however, your parents have a rule against any other kids driving their cars.

No . . .

Because . . .

But if . . .

You work at a fashionable clothing store. A friend wants you to "pick up" a particular jacket for him. He said, "It would be easy for you, and besides, your boss would never miss it."

No . . .

Because . . .

But if . . .

Your first period history teacher gives the same test each period. She uses the honor system to keep the questions secret from one class to the next. A friend asks you to tell her what is on the exam before she takes it fourth period.

No . . .

Because . . .

But if . . .

Your friends want you to be the lookout as they shoplift at a store in the mall.

No . . .

Because . . .

But if . . .

Prayer

Ask for God's help in learning how to express your love and concern for friends in a way which truly helps them.

Something for Later

USE THE FOLLOWING DEVOTIONAL THOUGHT THIS WEEK
AS YOU THINK ABOUT HAVING TO SAY NO IN TOUGH
SITUATIONS.

Saying no in uncomfortable situations is not easy. Read *Luke 4:1-13*. Luke describes the time right after Jesus' baptism, when He was tempted by Satan. Imagine turning down a chance to rule all you could see from a mountain top. Or, fasting for 40 days, but having to refuse food just because of the way you were to get it. Or imagine hang gliding without wings! Jesus had the chance to be caught and flown by angels, but He said no because He knew it wasn't right.

Jesus had studied God's Word and knew what it said. One major reason for having a quiet time is to learn what the Bible teaches about right and wrong. Jesus was already very clear on what was right and what was wrong before He was tempted. Trying to make up your mind while you are facing your friends is a lot harder. Having already thought through what is right is a big part of doing right.

This passage reminds us that no matter how wonderful your friend's suggestion to do wrong may sound, the result will not turn out so wonderfully. Jesus knew that if He accepted Satan's bargain, things would not go according to God's plan. He also knew there was not much chance things would turn out like Satan described. By accepting Satan's offer, Jesus would not have been the ruler of God's kingdom; instead, He would have become Satan's servant.

Ask God to give you the wisdom and courage to say no in His strength.

CASE STUDY: ROSA'S PROBLEM

Rosa has been kind of tense lately. She always seems ready to argue. She has been late to, or missed the last several meetings of the school newspaper and Spanish club. The worst part, though, seems to be the distance she has put between herself and her friends. She seems withdrawn.

Rosa confides in you. She tells you that she is having trouble at home. She wants to move out. She is seriously thinking about staying at a friend's house.

Her parents are down on her about the guy she is dating. Brad is fairly new in town. He works at a service station. He's good looking, but several years older than Rosa. He treats Rosa pretty good, but has a wild reputation.

Brad doesn't feel comfortable around adults, so he and Rosa have not spent any time around her parents. He still hasn't met them. When he picks her up, he blows the horn and she runs out to meet him.

Brad's name appeared in the paper refusing a blood-alcohol test. Now Rosa's parents have refused to let her see him. Rosa doesn't think it's fair."

Rosa admits that Brad drinks some, but claims he never gets drunk. "That night he had a couple of beers but not enough to affect his driving," she insists. "He's old enough to drink if he wants to, so what's the big deal? He doesn't try to make me drink, so what should it matter to my parents?"

Rosa and her parents have been in some heated arguments over this issue, with no end in sight. They have grounded her several times recently. They have demanded that she stop seeing Brad. Rosa has agreed, but they still meet secretly. Rosa lies to her mom to avoid a hassle.

But now the whole mess is eating her alive. She can't take the constant conflict. She asks for your advice.

How to Help Friends Work Through Their Problems

"He came to him, and bandaged up his wounds,
pouring oil and wine on them;
and he put him on his own beast,
and brought him to an inn, and took care of him"
(Luke 10:34).

GET A HANDLE ON IT

Keep the following three questions in mind as you try to gain insight into a problem your friend is dealing with:

1. What is the problem?
2. How does the problem occur?
3. What can be done about the problem?

WHAT IS THE PROBLEM?

The most important step in problem solving is finding out what the problem is. *But it's more important for your friend to identify the problem than it is for you to identify it.*

Measure the Impact

List all of the actions you think Rosa could take which may be helpful in resolving or reducing the conflict with her parents. Beside each action list the consequences or effects you think each action will have on Rosa and her parents.

Action	Effect on Rosa	Effect on her Parents
_____	_____	_____
_____	_____	_____
_____	_____	_____
_____	_____	_____
_____	_____	_____
_____	_____	_____
_____	_____	_____

Rosa needs to choose the action(s) with the most positive consequences, and fewest potentially negative effects, for all persons involved.

Jesus' Example as a Problem Solver

Because of His divine wisdom and His ability to listen so completely, Jesus was always able to get to the very heart of a *problem*. Look up the following Scripture passages and note the problem Jesus recognized.

Matthew 8:23-26

Matthew 9:1-4

Luke 10:38-42

Luke 12:13-15

Luke 24:36-38

John 20:26-29

EIGHT TRAPS TO AVOID IN PROBLEM SOLVING

1. Be sure to identify your friend's problem. Don't focus on someone else's problems.

Your friend must be willing to
that she has a _____.
This doesn't mean that the conflict is
your friend's _____.

2. Help your friend "own" the problem instead of blaming it on someone else.

Choose the answer below that best completes the sentence.

Helping a friend accept personal responsibility for
his problems is extremely difficult because:
    a. everyone wants to think they are blameless.
    b. few of us want to accept our own faults.
    c. of a condition called "moral
       accountability amnesia."
    d. all of the above.

3. Listen in a way that helps the friend understand his or her own feelings and the problem.

4. Do not try to be a professional therapist.

Plug in the seven words below so that the following five sentences make sense.

changed   care   unable

listen   professional   focus

overwhelmed

Your task is to_____with_____.
Try to help your friend_____on those things which can be_____or controlled.
Your friend may be_____to focus on the problem.
He may feel_____.
If this is the case, encourage_____counseling.

5. Be careful not to become emotionally burdened yourself.

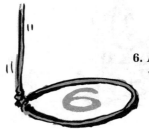

6. Avoid the tendency to do nothing to help while waiting.

7. Do not consider only the first option which was chosen long before any evaluation was made.

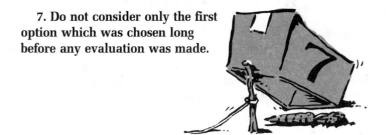

8. Don't take the responsibility away from your friend by doing everything for him.

WHAT CAN BE DONE?

There is always something positive your friend can do. No situation is hopeless. Realize that there are options that could benefit everyone involved.

After carefully considering each of the possible actions your friend may take, talk through the consequences of each action.

Read *2 Corinthians 1:3-4.* Praise God. Thank Him for being our ultimate helper.

Something for Later

USE THE FOLLOWING DEVOTIONAL THOUGHT THIS WEEK AS YOU LOOK FOR TIMES WHEN YOU CAN HELP YOUR FRIENDS.

GOOD SAMARITAN: GREAT EXAMPLE

Read *Luke 10:25-37*. Notice that not only was the Samaritan willing to get involved when others refused to *(vv. 31-33),* he did those things that he had the ability to do. He applied first aid *(v. 34),* he carried the victim to a place where he would be safe, his wounds could be tended, he could rest and be allowed to heal *(v. 34).* The Samaritan invested some time, energy, and, in this case, some money, in the man's treatment *(vv. 34-35).*

But, notice there were some things which he did not do. He did not stay with the man forever. He did not make the man dependent upon him. He did not try to perform surgery on the man. Instead, the Samaritan tried to get the man to the appropriate help.

How can following this example help you as you try to help your friends?

FREE COUNSELING AVAILABLE 24-HOURS A DAY

Local dignitaries have announced the opening of a new counseling center available free of charge. The center's Chief Executive Officer indicated that the service was to be free of charge and designed for immediate, easy access to the counselor.

The counselor, with years of experience in helping people work through the most difficult of life's problems, is described by many as being kind, compassionate, loving, and patient. Perhaps his most outstanding trait is the complete and thorough understanding of each and every problem clients have ever presented. No one has ever had to face a problem or conflict alone after having sought the professional help of our center's master therapist.

But even the references to counselor, professional, and master therapist seem strange in that the staff counselor is known for his "down to earth" genuineness which immediately puts one at ease.

Perhaps most important for our community's youth is the counselor's ability to relate to adolescents. Although not a young man, the counselor's understanding of today's youth and their problems is incredible. Quickly admitting that his teen years are long behind him, he acknowledges that he has remained in constant touch with teens in order to always be relevant to their current problems and needs.

How to Follow God as a Guide

*Even though I walk through
the valley of the shadow of death,
I fear no evil; for Thou art with me;
Thy rod and Thy staff, they comfort me
(Ps. 23:4).*

What's in a Name?

Every school has labels for the different groups that go there.
What type of person is being described by each label below?

ropers   dopers   nerds

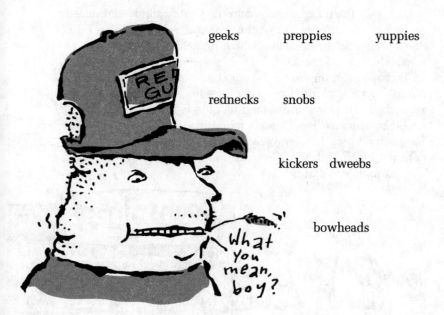

geeks   preppies   yuppies

rednecks   snobs

kickers   dweebs

bowheads

brains

jocks   wannabes

pets   hicks

Add other names that you
have heard applied to
different groups in your
school.

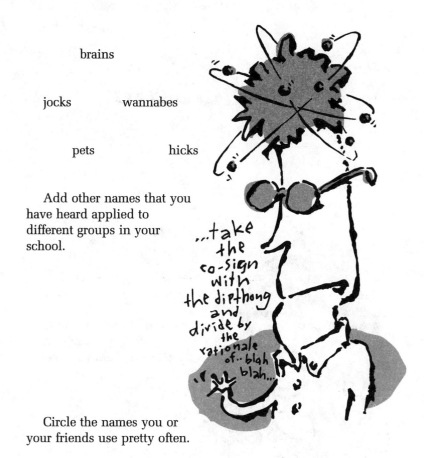

...take
the
co-sign
with
the dipthong
and
divide by
the
rationale
of.. blah
blah...

Circle the names you or
your friends use pretty often.

What is the name of the group(s) to which you belong?

What label would you least like to be called? Why?

Yoo hoo!

Do you think it is hard to truly care for people in groups very different from your own? Why?

GOD CARES

As a shepherd cares for his herd in the day when he is among his scattered sheep, so I will care for My sheep and will deliver them from all the places to which they were scattered on a cloudy and gloomy day (Ezek. 34:12).

Read *1 Peter 5:7*. Rewrite the verse in your own words.

God wants us to have a similar concern for others. Paul emphasized the concern we should have for each other. Read *1 Corinthians 12:24b-25*.

UNDERSTANDING AND WISDOM

Jesus has always understood you, even when you felt alone and misunderstood.

Several Bible passages tell us that Jesus paid attention to and understood the feelings of those He met.

In *Luke 5:1-11,* Jesus enlisted Peter, James, and John to be His followers. What emotion is mentioned in *verse 10?*

What do you think you would have been feeling if you had been there?

Locate *2 Chronicles 1:1-12* in your Bible. How did Solomon obtain wisdom?

Read *Psalm 11:10*. According to this verse, where does wisdom begin?

PATIENCE

Peter reminded early Christians of the patience of God, as He waited for Noah to build the ark *(1 Pet. 3:18-20)*.

Look up *Galatians 5:22-23*. When the Bible talks about the fruit of the Spirit, is it describing the fruit, or results, that the Holy Spirit brings about in believers' lives. God gives Christians patience.

FORGIVENESS

When you repent, you are asking God to forgive you. You are committing yourself to a different way of living.

1. Jesus knew God, His Father, was the source of forgiveness. Jesus prayed from the cross, *"Father forgive them; for they do not know what they are doing" (Luke 23:34a)*.

2. When Jesus taught His disciples to pray, He asked God to forgive them *(Matt. 6:12; Luke 11:4)*.

3. David knew that God was the source of forgiveness. Write the first half of *Psalm 130:4* in the space below.

4. Daniel knew that God was the source of forgiveness. See *Daniel 9:9* and write it below.

5. Paul also knew God was the source of forgiveness. Write in the space below what he told the people in one of his letters. (See *Eph. 4:32.*)

Ask God to help you forgive just as He has forgiven you.

Something for Later

Take time to do the following Bible Study this week. It will bring comfort to you and those God places in your life.

Read *John 14:1-31*. Place a bookmark there. You will want to turn to this passage often for comfort.

Jesus knew His followers were troubled *(v. 1)*. How did He try to help them in *verses 2-4?*

What do you think Thomas was feeling in *verse 5?*

Did Jesus try to put his mind at ease in *verses 6-7?*

Jesus understood that Philip still had not grasped everything. He tried to teach His followers *(vv. 8-10)*. Jesus carefully explained things once more *(vv. 11-21)*. Read these verses and write down what you think Philip was feeling.

When Judas (not the Judas who betrayed Jesus) asked a question, Jesus responded with understanding and compassion *(vv. 22-31)*. How do you think you might have felt if you had been there?

LOCAL CHURCH CONFUSES TEEN WITH "DOUBLE APPROACH"

ANY CITY, ANY TOWN — Billy B. Brown, an Any City High sophomore, was the focus between two disagreeing groups of youth at Local Baptist Church early last evening. In the pushing and taunting which followed, Brown was left confused and disheveled, wondering about the conflict.

According to the reports, Brown was caught between two different groups of friends in his church youth group. One group claimed to be Christians and carried large, leather-bound Bibles. They waved them in Brown's face and demanded that he follow the Bibles' teachings.

The other, much larger group also claimed to be Christians, but carried no Bibles. These youth indicated that Bibles were likely to offend their non-Christian friends, so they did not openly use Bibles.

In looking for the solution to a personal problem, Brown had sought the help of friends who quickly divided into the two disagreeing groups. Both groups were adamant about their positions.

According to Brown, "Whoa! Looks like there's bound to be something between these two ways. But, I still don't know what to do about my problem."

How to Use the Bible to Address Today's Problems

*All Scripture is inspired by God
and profitable for teaching,
for reproof, for correction, for training in righteousness;
that the man of God may be adequate,
equipped for every good work*
(2 Tim. 3:16-17, NIV).

Between the Lines

For each of the following persons, write what you think that person's approach to using the Bible would be—especially as it relates to Billy Brown's experience.

1. Pastor of local Baptist church

2. Friend of Billy Brown

3. Parent of one of the teenagers

4. Youth minister

5. High school teacher

Word Search

```
D N A T S R E D N U D N A W O N K R J V L
M C A B Q P L I V O Z G P N W R I O U I O
A O S R L G Z S D T O W D A D S O L M Q S
L N E E D F O R A C C E P T A N C E L A I
B F A D I S T E M P T E D A D A S O M H N
E L S O I C Q A H T C B B U M O S F F T G
S I S N C B X L K O X R C J F J O S E I S
U C U V O P V L I D W U K D A K Q C I W O
B T R I M I P Y R C H Y E N P N V R R E M
A W A E M S T M Y N J P O D V E J I G R E
G I N W A L E A F Z R P Q U Y V Y P T U T
U T C F N T S D U E K T J G L A T T L T H
R H E A D G O D S T L V C A W I O U E P I
D P O P M K A T T L I I J A M Q V R F I N
L A F F E G I E L A C S G M B J T E S R G
O R S X N O H D A D F N P E G P E A U C I
H E A C T X E B N V I Q G A G L R S S S M
O N L O S R R G O N F P Q Z R O J J E G P
C T V P I P A I N O F G U I L T F D J N O
L S A U N M P U J P Y Z E D K Z E O S I R
A T T Q M L R O V L H P N S Y I Q S M R T
I M I J I F Q Y E I E O D O Q D H P O A A
U N O A N X I E T Y A N D W O R R Y G H N
Z O N Q D L U O Y E K I L E N O E M O S T
Y R S T I L L E X P E R I E N C E F E A R
C M S E N O I S S E R P E D F O S E M I T
```

Use this list to find all 20 phrases.

WORD LIST

How You Live

Someone Like You

Role of Scripture

Those Trap Situations

Commandments in Mind

Alcohol Drug Abuse

Is Really Mad

Anxiety and Worry

Assurance of Salvation

Sharing Scripture With

Know and Understand

Jesus Felt Grief

Conflict with Parents

Pain of Guilt

Times of Depression

Losing Something Important

Still Experience Fear

Need for Acceptance

Running Away

Is Tempted

Scripture for Specific Problems

Using the Bible as your guide, record the help that each Scripture provides for each problem.

ALCOHOL OR DRUG ABUSE.—*(Rom. 12:1; 1 Cor. 6:19; Gen. 1:26; Prov. 20:1)*

ANGER.—*(Prov. 15:1; Eph. 4:26)*

ANXIETY AND WORRY.—*(Prov. 16:7;*
Matt. 6:25-27;
Matt. 6:34)

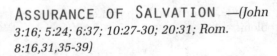

ASSURANCE OF SALVATION —*(John*
3:16; 5:24; 6:37; 10:27-30; 20:31; Rom.
8:16,31,35-39)

BEREAVEMENT AND DEATH.—*(John 11:1-46, particularly vv. 30-36; John 14; Psalm 23)*

CONFLICT WITH PARENTS.—*(2 Sam. 13–18; Matt. 7:12; Luke 6:31; Luke 15:11-32; Eph. 6:1-4)*

GUILT.—*(Rom. 8:1; Eph. 1:7)*

DEPRESSION.—*(Num. 11:10-15; 1 Kings 19:1-4; Job 3; Psalm 23; 27:14; Jer. 20; Jonah 4:3; Matt. 5:4; John 14:16-18)*

DISTRESS AND GRIEF.—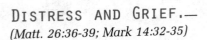
(Matt. 26:36-39; Mark 14:32-35)

FEAR.—*(Ps. 27:1; 56:11; 91:1-2; John 14:27; Phil. 4:19; Luke 22:41-44)*

NEED FOR ACCEPTANCE.—*(Gen. 37-50)*

RUNNING AWAY.—(also *Gen. 37-50)*

TEMPTATION.—*(Luke 4:1-13)*

Responding the Way Jesus Responds

What are some suggestions from Jesus' life that might help you as you respond to the needs of a friend? As you continue to help your friends, ask God to clearly reveal to you how Jesus would respond in each situation.

Something for Later

TAKE TIME THIS WEEK TO REALLY LOOK AT THE EXAMPLES OF LOVE AND FORGIVENESS IN THE FOLLOWING PASSAGE.

Read the story of the prodigal son in *Luke 15:11-32*.

How did guilt and forgiveness help to bring the parent and child back together?

What does this story tell you about God?

How can applying these principles change the way you relate to others, especially in difficult situations?

Now you should feel better equipped to help your friends.

Keep these five things in mind as you allow God to use you to make a difference in the lives of your friends:

First, sense when your friends have a problem, this means you must be a good listener and be able to identify signs of distress.

Second, you have to help your friends confront their problems. Also, this may be the time to use the **Three-Part No.**

Third, be available to help your friends work through their problems. Help them avoid Problem Solving Traps and then choose a correct plan of action.

Fourth, you must recognize and follow the Ultimate Guide, God, as you help your friends.

Fifth, use your best tool in helping your friends, the Bible.

Continue to grow in your dependence on the Lord. He will continue to lead you if you will follow Him.

A final reminder: don't expect to have all the answers. No one does other than God. Don't expect to solve all of the problems alone. None of us can. Trust God to help you help your friends.

Group Learning Activities

How to Sense Problems

Things You Need to Get

Two sheets of chart paper
Assorted colors of markers
14 sheets of 8 1/2-by-11-inch paper
Pencils
Extra Bibles

Things You Need to Do

Prepare two identical sets of the following six roadblock behaviors listed on pages 11-13 to be used in the "Dodging Roadblocks Matching Game": *Don't talk too much/Avoid overreacting/Don't be dishonest about your own feelings/Be sure you know yourself/Avoid being judgmental/Avoid excess advice.*

1. The Situation: The Fate of Chad Smith (10 minutes)

Read the story "RECENT SUICIDE LEAVES CONFUSION" from page 7. Say: **The story about Chad Smith's suicide is painful to think about. It may bother you because you have known someone who attempted or actually committed suicide. I'm sure you would have done anything to prevent the person from reaching such a hopeless point.**

Give each youth a copy of *How to Help Your Friends.* Say: **Get with a partner. One of you assume the role of Sue and the other the role of Warren. Discuss your feelings about this story. You have 120 seconds.**

Apologize for the short time by explaining that often we must assess a friend's crisis situation in even less time. We are "on call." Invite youth to tell Sue and Warren's feelings and their reasons for thinking so.

Be certain to mention that Warren and Sue probably felt some guilt or responsibility for Chad's death. Ask youth to share how they felt when they read Chad's story.

Point out that listening is the key to sensing problems.

2. What Did You Say? (10 minutes)

Invite youth to give 30-second testimonies about how a friend listened to them to sense a problem.

Interrupt the first person who shares. Look through your Bible and book as he speaks. Look around the room. Avoid making eye contact. When he finishes sharing ask: **Are you going to talk seriously to anyone who doesn't pay attention to you? Well, neither will your friends!** Allow others to share. Assure them that they will have your undivided attention.

Lay a sheet of chart paper and a marker in the center of the group. Ask a volunteer to write "A good listener . . ." on the paper, leaving space for written responses. Ask her to record responses from group members.

Direct youth to the section "What Did You Say?" Help youth find the answers by sharing: **Being *patient (answer 1)* in listening requires some conscious effort on our part. Sometimes it is hard to wait and let the one talking get to the point of the story.**

Ask a volunteer to read *Exodus 18:13* aloud. Ask youth to share the names of people who have Moses' job today.

Say: **If we are going to help someone by listening, we need to understand *(answer 2)* the problem and its related feelings and** issues. We need *wisdom (answer 3)* to recognize when we don't have the whole picture.

3. Wise Young Man (10 minutes)

Tell youth that helping friends is a skill that can improve daily. Remind youth that the Bible is a crucial source for use when helping their friends.

Say: **We can learn from each character in the Bible. A man named Solomon, though he had faults, was especially good at helping people solve problems.**

Ask youth to locate *1 Kings 3:7-28* in their Bibles. Ask volunteers to use their Bibles as scripts and read the roles of Solomon *(vv. 7-9,15-16,23-25,27)*, God *(vv. 10-14)*, the first woman *(vv. 17-21,22b,22c,26)*, the second woman *(vv. 22a,22c,25,26b,27)*, and the amazed Israelites *(v. 28)*.

Ask youth to answer the first three questions under the section "Wise Young Man" on page 10. Lead youth to discuss why they feel Solomon made a wise ruling. Then say: **Some of your friends may have talked with you about a tough problem. Without mentioning any names, tell about the toughest decision you have helped a friend make? Did you offer good advice? What was your advice?**

Ask youth to record in the space provided the advice they offered. Encourage youth to share. Read *Proverbs 25:11-12* from a Bible or from page 11.

4. Slow to Speak (5 minutes)

Do not say anything following this activity. Wait until someone breaks the silence by speaking. Ask: **Was it awkward to sit in silence? Have you noticed times when a group becomes quiet and talking fades into silence? Someone always jumps in with a comment that refocuses the group's attention. Some people — but not all — may interrupt because they are uncomfortable with the silence. Sometimes we need to risk being *silent (answer 4)*. Try not to make a friend uncomfortable during a serious conversation by refusing to speak, but give him** a chance to talk. Allow time for your friend to think — perhaps cry— without interrupting.

5. Riding the Roller Coaster (10 minutes)

Say: **Your emotions are like a roller coaster. God created us to be emotional creatures — especially during the teen years. But some emotional behaviors occur too often. These frequent or constant moods serve as warning flags that something may be wrong.**

Place a sheet of chart paper in the center of the group. Use markers to draw a roller coaster. Title the poster "Riding the Roller Coaster: Five Signs of Distress." Ask a volunteer to plot each distress sign as it is discussed. Ask youth to give an example of each sign. Record their examples. Share the following so youth can record responses:

◆ *Acting out* is a psychological term that describes *the behavior of an angry person who responds to the anger by trying to hurt someone or something.* Guys your age may "act out" by *fighting.* When a person deals with hurt, frustration, conflict, embarrassment, or anger by striking out at someone or something, those aggressive actions are often the signals of their inner hurt.

◆ Watch for friends who begin to *withdraw* from persons and activities they once enjoyed. *This is more than being shy.*

◆ Remember: *Sudden, unexplained mood swings* are distress signals. There may be a problem *if the swings are larger and more frequent than those of your other friends.*

◆ Stop and ask youth to rank the ten *Major life problems* on page 15. Discuss how and why youth ranked the events. Say: **Everyone has problems. But some problems may cause a friend to need help from you or perhaps from a professional counselor.** Some youth really struggle with events that other youth blow off.

◆ Perhaps the foremost warning sign that counselors or psychologists look for is *depression. Depression* is a warning sign whenever *it hangs on for days and prevents a person from keeping up with typical activities.* Encourage youth to notice those times when friends seem particularly depressed. If that mood continues for more than a week or two without relief, your friend may need help.

6. Dodging Roadblocks Matching Game (10 minutes)

Place the 12 roadblock behavior answers that you prepared earlier number-side-up on the floor. Ask the person who has the longest last name to begin the game by selecting two of the sheets of paper by calling out two numbers. If a match is made, she continues until she misses. If a match is not made, play passes to the person on her left.

As a match is made discuss its importance. Encourage youth to take notes in the margin on page 11.

Say: **Sometimes a person can be a barrier to communication.** Ask youth to record in the space provided a time when they were a barrier to communication

7. Prayer - Friends Hurting in Silence (5 minutes)

Ask youth to share their answers to the two jumbled phrases on page 8. Say: **By now you probably have discovered the most important characteristic of a friendship. You learned that "insignswell ot phel" is really "willingness to help."**

The first step in the process of being able to help others: "sensing that there is a problem." Not only is this the first step, and maybe the most important, it may be the hardest. Because sometimes certain problems are never discussed – even with a close friend.

Ask youth to think about friends who are hurting in silence. Ask youth to use the space provided to write a prayer to God.

Close with a group prayer, thanking God for listening and helping us to help our friends. Challenge youth to choose to do "Something for Later" on page 17.

How to Confront Problems

Things You Need to Get

Two sheets of chart paper
Markers
Pencils
Extra Bibles

Things You Need to Do

Enlist an older male to share the following monologue. Encourage him to tell it like it happened to him.

Last year, six of us guys were riding in a friend's car. Someone had the bright idea for all of us to sway our bodies, left and right, to see if we could rock the car enough to turn it over from the inside. Get the picture?—six guys in a car going 40 miles per hour, rocking. The car swerved left on two wheels, then right, back and forth across the two-lane highway.

I was in the middle of the front seat. I knew we were going to turn over. BUT I NEVER SAID A WORD. I wish I had had the nerve to tell the guys that it was stupid. That we could get killed.

But I didn't say anything. I didn't confront the problem. Lucky for us, we didn't have an accident. I was really afraid of that. But, I was more afraid of being laughed at by my friends for being "chicken." There is definitely some risk in confronting your friends.

Prepare a poster with the heading "THREE-PART NO" and the following points: (1) Say "NO!" rather than any other phrase that could be taken the wrong way. (2) Tell your friend why. (3) Finally, if there is something you can do to help your friend, be sure to say what that is.

1. The Situation: Help! Erica Brown Is in Trouble
   (10 minutes)

Ask: **Does your school or youth group have any kind of effort in which students take responsibility for helping solve the problems fellow students face?**

Share that if any active effort to help is ever offered, it is probably provided by adults, or by some social agency. Direct youth to the section "Help!" on page 19. Allow time for youth to evaluate each issue and discuss their involvement (and that of their school and church groups), if any, in each.

Say: **Listen as I tell you about a friend that you may know. Her name might be different. Or "she" may be a "he." She has a problem. See if you can help.**

After reading the case study. Discuss possible solutions to Erica's problem. Ask: **What could a school or youth group do to help Erica?**

2. To Confront, or Not to Confront? (5 minutes)

Invite youth to name the first word that pops in their minds when they hear the word *confront*. Write these on a sheet of chart paper.

Invite the enlisted youth to share his story by saying: **(Youth's name) was telling me about a situation that relates to our discussion. He said that he wouldn't mind sharing it with the group.**

After he finishes. Ask youth what they would have done in the situation. Say: **This incident never really happened but it could have. What situations have you been in where you had to make the decision "to confront or not to confront?"**

Guide youth to see confrontation as a tool of love, not power.

3. Three Things You Might Confront (10 minutes)

Ask a volunteer to read Confrontation 1 on page 20. Tell youth that they have just discussed this first confrontation. Invite youth to write in the space provided any notes that will help them deal with this type of confrontation.

Ask another volunteer to read Confrontation 2. Guide discussion by sharing that addiction to alcohol or drugs is sometimes seen as a way out. Warn youth to not act in a way that helps the addiction to continue (lying to cover for a friend, giving homework to a friend to copy when you knew she had been drinking heavily the night before). These actions *enable the addiction* (make it possible).

Ask another volunteer to read Confrontation 3. Guide discussion by asking youth to think about the number of times Christ confronted the unfair attitudes of those around Him. Challenge youth to read through the Gospels. Tell youth that they will be impressed with the many times Jesus confronted both friend and enemy. Each time, He did so in an effort to help the person grow and improve.

4. Jesus Spoke Up (10 minutes)

Assign each youth one of the six Scripture passages from page 21. Double up if you need to. Allow time for youth to discover the persons and problems Jesus confronted in each situation and record responses. Invite youth to share with the entire group. Ask youth to notice attitudes and actions Jesus used.

Ask youth to choose the best answer to the multiple-choice question on page 22 (*d. all of the above*).

5. Two More Things You Might Confront (10 minutes)

Divide the group into two groups. Make the following assignments:

Group 1 - Confrontation 4
Read the Scripture and respond to the question under "A Very Ugly Story" on page 22.

Group 2 - Confrontation 5
Poll the entire group and prepare a statement based on your findings of those youth who lash back and those who quickly withdraw when "chewed out" (page 23). Then, share personal examples that support Jesus' instructions in *Matthew 18:15a*.

Allow time for each group to share. After the first group finishes share that *2 Samuel 11,* tells how King David used his powerful position to have an adulterous affair, conceive a child, and then have the woman's husband killed. The way the chapter ends suggests David's arrogance as he covered up his deed. *Second Samuel 12:1-11* describes how Nathan confronted David's problem head-on.

Share that denial is a common part of how people try to cope with life's biggest problems. Your friend's denial is a chance for you to confront the real problem and help him.

6. Three-Part No (15 minutes)

Ask, **When was it the toughest to say no to a friend?** Allow responses and then say, **Those are always bad situations. One way to stay out of a bad situation is to adopt the Three-Part No. To try it, follow these three steps:**

Reveal the "THREE-PART NO" poster you have prepared. Call on a volunteer to read the first statement. Invite discussion and then respond, **Don't say "Maybe," or "Let me think about it," or "Well, I don't really want to." Because you don't want to hurt your friend's feelings, you may have a tendency to avoid using the word *no,* but you must.**

Have another youth read the second statement. After discussion say, **Honestly explain your reason. Say something like, "No, Bill, I really can't do that for you because I don't think it is right (or whatever is your honest reason)." You know how you feel when parents or teachers tell you no without giving you a reason. You may not always like or agree with the reason you get, but you feel better if you have at least heard the reason.**

Read the third statement. After discussion add, **Say "No, I can't help you during the test tomorrow because I don't believe in cheating; but, I would help you study after school today if you'd like." There may not be anything you can do to help, but if there is, and you feel like it fits, then say so.**

Say, **The Three-Part No can be thought of in these words** (write the following on the chart paper as you talk). **No, because . . ., but if . . . . Try it, you may find it helpful.**

Discuss as a large group the four case studies on pages 24-27. Ask youth to write a Three-Part No to each case study as it is discussed.

Say: **One of the best ways to confront problems is to stand up for what is right. Jesus is our best model for this. Pray, thanking God for showing you how to confront problems.** Challenge youth to choose to do "Something for Later" on page 29.

Session 3

How to Help Friends Work Through Their Problems

Things You Need to Get

18 sheets of 8 1/2-by-11-inch paper
One sheet of lined paper for each youth
Two sheets of chart paper
Markers
Pencils
Extra Bibles

Things You Need to Do

Draw 9 X's and 9 O's on paper and put some tape on the back of each.

Make a poster entitled "THE SIX A'S." Under the title, list the following six statements. Write the A's in bold:

Admit—What questions or actions will you take to guide the friend to own this problem?

Ask hard questions—What can you ask to help your friend understand and solve the problem?

Another to help—What adult could give you or your friend guidance in solving the problem?

Accept responsibility—How will you help your friend discover how the problem works and how s/he controls in it?

Act with maturity—How will you help your friend see what she contributes to the problem and change damaging actions?

Action Plan—How will you help your friend develop and carry out actions that will solve the problem or at least minimize it?

HOW TO HELP FRIENDS WORK THROUGH THEIR PROBLEMS

77

1. The Situation: Rosa's Problem (15 minutes)

Direct all youth to open *How to Help Your Friends* to page 30 and follow along as you read "CASE STUDY: ROSA'S PROBLEM." Ask youth to complete "Measure the Impact" on page 32.

Assign half of the group to be the O team and the remaining half to be the X team. Set chairs in three rows of three to form a human size tic-tac-toe board.

Call for an X to come to the nine chairs, choose the chair he wants to mark for a tic-tac-toe, and sit in it. If he answers correctly he stays in the chair. If he misses, any O can answer. If you have less than nine youth, they leave their X's in the chairs after answering. Ask the following questions (allow credit for thoughtful answers.)

1. Recently Rosa has been tense, argumentative, withdrawn, and her school work has declined. How has her problem contributed to these results?
2. How has Rosa's behavior actually caused her problems?
3. How has Rosa tried to talk with her parents?
4. How much older is Brad, and what attracts Rosa to him?
5. As Rosa describes Brad there are many "buts" in the description. Why?
6. What is it about the relationship with Brad that makes being dishonest with Rosa's parents OK?
7. Identify one problem you see in Rosa's situation *(can ask this many times)*.
8. Restate an item on Rosa's list to be her problem, not another's? *(can ask this many times)*.
9. To start working out Rosa's problem, what must she do? *(own it, admit she has a problem)*.
10. Do you think Rosa's problem started with her parents or dating a not-good-for-her guy and why? *(either but urge reasons)*.
11. Why be honest when Rosa decides to secretly see her boyfriend? *(lying always hurts)*.

2. Jesus' Example as a Problem Solver (10 minutes)

Ask youth to choose one of the six Scripture passages from page 33. Ask youth to search the passage to find the problem that Jesus identified. Suggest they work in pairs. Allow time to share.

3. Eight Traps to Avoid in Problem Solving (15 minutes)

Give every youth a sheet of paper and guide each to draw some type of trap (mousetrap, bear trap, etc.) Have youth write on the trap abbreviated versions of the eight traps from pages 34-38. Ask: **Which trap are you most likely to get caught in? What injury happens or has happened when you're in this trap? How do or will you escape? What actions, words and attitudes keep you from walking into the trap?**

As each trap is discussed, comment on the material included and/or respond to the related questions, if any. *(Answers: TRAP 1. admit, problem, fault; TRAP 2. a and b; TRAP 3. No questions; TRAP 4. Your task is to listen with care. Try to help your friend focus on those things which can be changed or controlled. Your friend may be unable to focus on the problem. He may feel overwhelmed. If this is the case, encourage professional counseling; TRAPS 5, 6, 7, 8. No material or questions.)*

4. Real Life Case Studies (15 minutes)

Ask youth to think about a real problem they or a friend are facing. Ask youth not to reveal names of friends or share intimate details. Give each youth a piece of lined paper. Ask them to write down the problem. Reveal The Six A's Poster.

Ask youth to exchange case studies. As a group use the Six A's to solve the problems presented.

Ask: **Why should you help your friend solve the problem, instead of solving it yourself?** *(Examples: Friend has to carry out solution; friend must change actions; friend may blame you if it doesn't work out; more).* Encourage youth to apply the questions from page 31 to any situation that requires more information for better understanding.

5. Prayer (5 minutes)

Focus on God as the ultimate helper. Enlist a youth to read *2 Corinthians 1:3-4*. Then lead a time of praising and thanking God. Challenge youth to choose to do "Something for Later" on page 40.

How to Follow God As A Guide

Things You Need to Get
Markers
4 sheets of 8 1/2-by-11-inch paper
One sheet of tinfoil for each youth
One paper clip for each youth
Pencils
Extra Bibles

Things You Need to Do
Make small posters of the following verses by writing each on a separate sheet of paper:

For a child will be born to us, a son will be given to us; and the government will rest on His shoulders; and His name will be called Wonderful Counselor. . . . (Isa. 9:6a).

He came to Jesus at night and said, "Rabbi, we know you are a teacher who has come from God. For no one could perform the miraculous signs you are doing if God were not with him" (John 3:2, NIV).

Jesus therefore answered them, "My teaching is not Mine, but His who sent me" (John 7:16).

"The Counselor, the Holy Spirit, whom the Father will send in my name, will teach you all things and will remind you of everything I have said to you" (John 14:26, NIV).

1. The Situation: Free Counseling Available (10 minutes)
Ask youth to read and respond to the article "Free Counseling Available 24-Hours

a Day" on page 41. Ask, **Have you ever known anyone like the staff counselor who is mentioned in the article?**

Hold up the four Scripture posters one at at time. Call on volunteers to read each one as you hold it up. After the last Scripture is read say: **The counselor described is of course Jesus Himself.** Jesus lived a life which can be a ready model for each of us as we try to be helpers. The Holy Spirit exists today as a ready Counselor for all Christians. Through the Holy Spirit, you can have the daily guidance and teaching necessary to grow more like Him. **We become friends to our friends as we imitate Jesus.**

2. The Ideal Counselor (10 minutes)

Direct youth to sculpt the ideal friend/helper. Provide foil. As youth report highlight Christlike qualities in their presentations. Ask: **What makes a good friend/helper? What bugs you about the way some friends help? How does God want you to improve your friend helping?**

3. What's In a Name? (10 minutes)

Share that we don't always imitate Jesus, and that we especially betray Him in the names we call each other. Complete "What's in a Name?" on pages 42-43 as a group. Answer all of the questions aloud.

Give each youth a paper clip and direct them to bend it into what these names do to people. Invite each youth to choose one label they feel is most unlike them and then to write in the margin of their book five ways they are like the people being described.

As youth name similarities direct all to make a paper clip chain. As the group does this say, **Actions can link persons to persons and persons to God.**

4. God Cares (10 minutes)

Read *Ezekiel 34:12* on page 45. Then ask youth to locate *1 Peter 5:7* in their Bibles and rewrite the verse in their own words in the space provided. Share that this verse tells us to turn our anxiety over to God because He cares for us. We are to depend upon God's concern for us. By depending upon Him, we are able to overcome our anxieties.

Say, **God wants us to care for others the way He cares for us.** Ask a volunteer to read *1 Corinthians 12:24b-25.*

Recall that God Himself is the source of our salvation, friends' salvation, and the solutions to our problems. Call on volunteers to tell how to be and live as a Christian using "Something You Need to Know" on the back inside cover of this book and an object in the room. *(Example: Living as a Christian is like a plug because as we plug our actions and attitudes into Him we get power to enjoy life).*

5. Traits to Adopt (15 minutes)

Ask youth to get in groups of twos or threes. Assign one of the following sections to each group: "Understanding and Wisdom;" "Patience;" "Forgiveness." Ask youth to complete the material in their assigned section and then share with the entire group.

6. Prayer (5 minutes)

Say: **You decide how good a friend/helper you will be. It's not something you have or don't have. It's something you choose. Begin by linking up with God and then imitate Him in word, action, attitude.**

Direct youth to pray for the person on their left and then right, to choose to love people through God-honoring words and actions. Challenge youth to choose to do "Something for Later" on pages 50-51.

How to use the Bible to Address Today's Problems

Things You Need to Get
Pencils
Extra Bibles

Things You Need to Do
Review the 13 problems and related Scriptures on pages 55-59 so that you will be prepared to guide discussion during the activity, "Scripture for Specific Problems."

1. The Situation: Local Church Confuses Teen (10 minutes)
Read "Local Church Confuses Teen with "Double Approach" from page 52. Assign one of the five persons listed under "Between the Lines" on pages 53-54 to each youth. Have youth record how they feel each person would

approach Billy's problem and then share it with the entire group.

Say: **Well, Billy Brown is right. There has got to be a way to live your faith and honor God's Word without hiding the truth or scaring people off before they can be helped. Let's begin to look for that better way.**

A place to start is how you live. Letting others see how Jesus' influence has changed you gives them a better idea of who Jesus is. When you try to help your friends, Jesus will guide you.

2. Word Search (10 minutes)

Give each youth a pencil and ask them to complete the word search on page 54. Say: **Each phrase has three words except "running away" and "is tempted" which have two.** Ask youth to use the word list following the puzzle as their guide. Call for each phrase in the order it appears in the list and ask youth to relate it to the subject of helping friends. Accept any positive response. (A copy of the solved puzzle appears on page 92.)

3. Word Search (10 minutes)

Have youth silently read *Matthew 22:33-40*. Ask youth to share how Jesus used Scripture in this situation.

Share that it helps to know and understand what God's Word has to say on an issue. Then you can offer those insights at a time and in a way that your friend can understand.

4. Scripture for Specific Problems (25 minutes)

Ask a volunteer to read the 13 problems listed on pages 55-59. Invite youth to work alone, in pairs, or as a large group to relate Scripture to the list of problems. Point out that the Scriptures used are not the only ones that apply. Challenge youth to locate additional Scriptures. Spend half of the time working and the other half discussing each problem.

Use the following information to help in your discussion. Adapt as necessary.

Alcohol or Drug Abuse.—Our bodies are to be kept healthy as temples for God's Spirit *(Rom. 12:1; 1 Cor. 6:19)*. There are also Scriptures that warn of the affects of using alcoholic beverages *(Prov. 20:1)*. God made us all in His image and we must respect all that His Word says about how we are meant to be *(Gen. 1:26)*.

Anger.—It pays to remain calm and soft-spoken *(Prov. 15:1)*. Anger is an emotion; but what an angry person does may be a sin. We are responsible for our behavior. A good way to get past angry feelings is to put that energy into working out the problem as best we can *(Eph. 4:26)*.

Anxiety and Worry.—It's hard to just concentrate on trying to do what God would have us do and let Him take care of the rest *(Prov. 16:7)*. I think we all tend to worry about things we can't do anything about instead of focusing on what we could do *(Matt. 6:25-27,34)*.

Assurance of Salvation.—If you or your friends ever have doubts, I encourage you to read the following passages in *John 3:16; 5:24; 6:37; 10:27-30; 20:31,* and *Romans 8:16,31,35-39.* These are not all the reassuring verses, by any means. But these are some of my favorites. If you need extra help, please talk to your pastor or youth leader.

Bereavement and Death.—Nothing is more natural than grieving over the death of a loved one. Even Jesus felt grief *(John 11:1-46,* particularly *vv. 30-36)*. Just being able to be with a friend who cares and will listen is a big comfort. *Psalm 23* is a comforting Scripture passage; share it with your friend. *John 14* is a source of great comfort to many.

Conflict with Parents.—The bitter conflict between King David and his son, Absalom, thousands of years ago, is described in the Old Testament *(2 Sam. 13–18)*. In the New Testament, there is a story many people know as the story of the prodigal son *(Luke 15:11-32)*. It is important that it teaches parents to be lovingly open to their children *(v. 20)*, and that children should ask for forgiveness when they are wrong *(v. 21)*. Another good thought from the Bible that applies to better family relationships is to treat our parents the way we would like to be treated *(Luke 6:31;*

Matt. 7:12). Children should also honor and respect their parents, obeying them unless told to do something immoral *(Eph. 6:1-3).* Parents should avoid exasperating their children and train them as God would want *(Eph. 6:4).*

Guilt.—No one has escaped the pain of guilt. Nobody likes feeling guilty. However, guilt, like fear, serves a purpose. Feeling guilty can cause us to seek God. When you confess and repent, God is faithful to forgive us *(Rom. 8:1; Eph. 1:7).* Forgiveness overcomes guilt, but others may not be as willing as God to forgive us.

To remove guilt, first, ask forgiveness from God and from anyone we have hurt. Try to right the wrong. Do whatever is possible to right the wrong.

Depression.—Many great heroes in the Bible experienced times of depression. Moses *(Num. 11:10-15),* Job *(Job 3),* Elijah *(1 Kings 19:1-4),* Jonah *(Jonah 4:3),* and Jeremiah *(Jer. 20)* are a few that come to mind. No matter how down you feel, others have felt the same way and gone on to prosper.

The Bible can be a great tool for giving strength. Verses such as, *Psalm 23; 27:14; Matthew 5:4; John 14:16-18,* are only a few of the verses that can help improve the outlook. But, if depression lingers and interrupts daily activity, seeing a counselor or physician should be encouraged. Depression can actually change a person's body chemistry to the point of becoming an illness.

Distress and Grief.—Grief is not just the emotion felt when someone close to you dies. Grief can be experienced anytime someone goes through losing something important: breaking up with a girlfriend or boyfriend; moving to another town; an injury that keeps you out of usual activities; a disaster that destroys your home.

Jesus felt grief and distress *(Matt. 26:36-39; Mark 14:32-35).* When He did, He wanted friends to get away with Him to pray.

Fear.—Even if we are Christians and have God with us *(Ps. 27:1; 56:11; 91:1-2; John 14:27; Phil. 4:19),* we may still experience fear. Some fears are good in that they help us avoid danger. Because some fears actually serve to protect us, the emotion itself doesn't seem to me to be the problem. Having a life dominated by fear that freezes our ability to function is a problem. Jesus had every reason to be afraid while he was in the Garden of Gethsemane. He was about to be betrayed to the Romans by His friend, Judas. But notice what He did in that fearful hour. He prayed *(Luke 22:41-44)*.

Need for Acceptance.—Joseph *(See Gen. 37-50)* was his father's favorite. This naturally bothered his brothers. He also reported having dreams about ruling over his brothers. When Joseph was 17, his brothers hated him so much that they wanted to kill him. They sold Joseph to some traders who took him to Egypt as a slave.

Joseph worked hard and did a good job in what he was given to do. He worshiped God instead of blaming Him for what had happened. God blessed him when his brothers would not. Joseph forgave his brothers long before they ever asked for forgiveness, thus he avoided becoming bitter. Finally, he reached out to his brothers instead of demanding that they reach for him.

Running Away.—Joseph was thrown away by his family. You may have a friend who has either been thrown out or run away from home.

If you have a friend who has run away, try convincing him to let his parents know where he is, or at least that he is safe. Encourage your friend to avoid trying to get back at his parents by making them worry more. Encourage your friend to find some way to talk to his or her parents. Consider asking an adult friend, pastor, teacher, or someone else who could help set up the possibility for your friend and parents to start communicating.

Temptation.—Jesus dealt with temptation *(Luke 4:1-13).* You and your friends have too. Suppose a close friend confides in you that she is tempted to do something that you both agree is wrong. The friend is desperate to pass the math final. If your friend can make a high B on the test, she will get a passing grade for the course. Unfortunately, C+ is the highest grade your friend has ever earned in math. She has studied but still doesn't know the material.

Your friend has learned of a way to steal a copy of the test. Neither of you want to steal or cheat, but the temptation of a guaranteed A is so strong! What do you do?

5. Prayer (5 minutes)

Invite youth to share their favorite Bible verse for helping friends. Spend some time in prayer thanking God for His wisdom and asking for guidance as they help their friends. Challenge youth to choose to do "Something for Later" on pages 60-61.

(Solution to Word Search on page 54.)

```
D N A T S R E D N U D N A W O N K R J V L
M C A B Q P L I V O Z G P N W R I O U I O
A O S R L G Z S D T O W D A D S O L M Q S
L N E E D F O R A C C E P T A N C E L A I
B F A D I S T E M P T E D A D A S O M H N
E L S O I C Q A H T C B B U M O S F F T G
S I S N C B X L K O X R C J F J O S E I S
U C U V O P V L I D W U K D A K Q C I W O
B T R I M I P Y R C H Y E N P N V R I E M
A W A E M S T M Y N J P O D V E J I G R E
G I N W A L E A F Z R P Q U V V Y P T U T
U T C F N T S D U E K T J G L A T T L T H
R H E A D G O D S T L V C A W I O U E P I
D P O P M K A T T L I I J A M Q V R F I N
L A F F E G I E L A C S G M B J T E S R G
O R S X N O H D A D F N P E G P E A U C I
H E A C T X E B N V I Q G A G L R S S S M
O N L O S R R G O N F P Q Z R O J J E G P
C T V P I P A I N O F G U I L T F D J N O
L S A U N M P U J P Y Z E D K Z E O S I R
A T T Q M L R O V L H P N S Y I Q S M R T
I M I J I F Q Y E I E O D O Q D H P O A A
U N O A N X I E T Y A N D W O R R Y G H N
Z O N Q D L U O Y E K I L E N O E M O S T
Y R S T I L L E X P E R I E N C E F E A R
C M S E N O I S S E R P E D F O S E M I T
```

Christian Growth Study Plan

Preparing Christians to Grow

In the **Christian Growth Study Plan (formerly Church Study Course),** this book *How to Help Your Friends, Revised* is a resource for course credit in the subject area Ministry of the Christian Growth category of diploma plans. To receive credit, read the book, complete the learning activities, show your work to your pastor, youth minister or church leader, then complete the information on the next page.

Send the completed page to the Christian Growth Study Plan, 127 Ninth Avenue, North, MSN 117, Nashville, TN 37234-0117. This page may be duplicated. FAX: (615)251-5067

For information about the Christian Growth Study Plan, refer to the current Christian Growth Study Plan Catalog. Your church office may have a copy. If not, request a free copy from the Christian Growth Study Plan office (615/251-2525).

How to Help Your Friends, Revised
CG-0134

PARTICIPANT INFORMATION

Social Security Number		Personal CGSP Number*	Home Phone	Date of Birth	
— — —			— —	— —	

Name (First, MI, Last)
☐ Mr. ☐ Miss
☐ Mrs.

Address (Street, Route, or P. O. Box) | City, State | Zip Code

CHURCH INFORMATION

Church Name

Address (Street, Route, or P. O. Box) | City, State | Zip Code

CHANGE REQUEST ONLY

☐ Former Name

☐ Former Address | City, State | Zip Code

☐ Former Church | | Zip Code

Signature of Pastor, Conference Leader, or Other Church Leader | Date

*New participants are requested but not required to give SS# and date of birth. Existing participants, please give CGSP# when using SS# for the first time. Thereafter, only one ID# is required. Mail to: Christian Growth Study Plan, 127 Ninth Ave., North, MSN 117, Nashville, TN 37234-0117. Fax: (615)251-5067